Satellite View

poems by

Lance Newman

Finishing Line Press
Georgetown, Kentucky

Satellite View

ACKNOWLEDGMENTS

Several of the poems in this chapbook appeared in the following places:

Breadbox Parsons: "Baghdad Swing."
Dark Mountain Project: "Dream of Fog" and "Facing West from California's
    Shores."
El Portal: "Another Albuquerque Job" and "Anza Borrego."
Negative Images: "After the Fires" and "Horizon."
nthposition: "Commencement," "Dream of Flight" and "What's New at
    Home?"
Streetnotes: "Convenience," "Corrales Rancho Homes," "Miramar," and
    "Temple Square."
Stride: "Variations on My Life."
Zyzzyva: "Cerro de las Posas," "Don't Call My Cell," and "Dream of Frost in
    Boston."

Publisher: Leah Huete de Maines
Editor: Christen Kincaid
Cover Art: Lance Newman
Author Photo: Freya Newman
Cover Design: Elizabeth Maines McCleavy

Order online: www.finishinglinepress.com
          also available on amazon.com

Author inquiries and mail orders:
Finishing Line Press
PO Box 1626
Georgetown, Kentucky 40324
USA

Contents

For A. McA. Miller

Dream of Hindsight

At the treeless heart of summer
there was a crevice darted with nests
in a cup of volcanic glass.
The piano wings of vultures
tilted through a creosote playground.
Once I saw cliffrose in winter
by a frozen creek where an owl
treasured carrion in the snow.
Under the swift razor of ice
miles of piñons and cedars
shuddered for an ordinary wind,
a last flake of snow, a slender
hawk attending to hummingbirds
in an explosion of primrose.

Temple Square

The sun rises bright as a salesman, so
bright the mountains look black. Asphalt gleams
like ice. For fifteen shining minutes
at dawn, you can hear pigeons preening.
Mirrored storefronts burn like searchlights
on sidewalks clean as diner counters.
The dry breeze smells like sand. For fifteen
minutes before the engines start,
no one moves. No one speaks. Newspapers
lay stacked in boxes. Eggs rest in crates.
This is the time the day is weakest.
If the *Trib* asked, "Why?" above the fold,
we'd lay down our brushes, walk out the door
in our robes, and sit down on the curb.

What's New at Home?

The city fixed that pipe and paved our block.
Now when the street sweeper leaves a snail
track around the deli van, the fresh
blacktop glows silver as glass under blue
halogen light. Just two weeks since Delta
flew you to Phoenix, but everything's new
since you left. Get this. The city dashed
our fire hydrant with dalmatian spots.
Then yesterday some punk wheat-pasted
the grey telecom box back and front
with Andre the Giant. *Obey*. Still.
The super raked the butts and ashes,
planted cabbage by our maple sapling.
Four malt-liquor tallboys in twisted
sacks hold up a wall like a rank of thugs.
A shrink-wrapped stack of battered pallets
waits for Monday on the American
Fulfillment Company's loading dock.
Guess what. I can bootleg their wifi
from our stoop. Our coffee shop won't roll
up its shutters till eight. Next door three shoes
lounge like centerfolds on mustard taffeta.
The cash machine plays CNN headlines
and the anchor's clearly sure the blast
was accidental. Sure. Bye now.
Please click reply to all.

Mill Creek Canyon

Jersey barriers hem in the fee booth
and there's a flagger ahead. *Speed Limit 30.*

Power lines festoon poles soaked in creosote.
No Parking Any Time by drought-killed
box elders and Gambel oaks.

Green weeds line the cracked asphalt
but dry fuel stands in ranks to the ridges.

A downbound Tesla stirs leaf litter
on the fog line. Meteorology
rides shotgun and the dashcam scrolls dust.

Where's that atmospheric river now?
Digital nomads won't do the trick.

A bridge sports flagstone swerve-guards,
as if I'm looking for a spot to roll
into the creek's last trickle of snowmelt.

I've never thought about smoke
crossing state lines in darkness.

Once upon a time a spiky
limestone ridge rose like a cake
over the creek's jangly froth.

I'll always *Be Prepared to Stop*
for an avalanche of dry scree,

and sure, I'll *Drown Campfires Dead Out,*
forever in a work zone
where fines are doubled.

Dream of State Street

The redbuds in the park strip show
blood orange over a couple
nodding out on a traffic-calming
bump out. Shouldn't it be shelter weather?
There used to be a body shop,
a wrecking yard and a deli
where now a work crew is rushing up
another row of boxy condos.
Today I'm interchangeable
as electrons, locked in orbit
around the dispensary's drive-thru.
I amble from one second to the next
till it's another degree hotter
and everything's changed places again.

Miramar

National security moms
bray at yellow ribbon parties.

One lectures: The Milky Way
shows God's blood, sweat, and tears.

Red, white, and blue bunting
swathes the flat plasma TV.

She pats out hamburgers
and greases a skillet

for some grunt sitting high
as a knight in his raked truck.

He's got his game face on
and vanity tags: *CHAMP*.

His tailgate reads *Jet Noise,*
the Sound of Freedom. Chump.

Don't Call My Cell

I hoped the blaze would crap out on the ridge.
It exploded the tower's batteries & now
our block is a dead zone. I balanced between
skulking to town to text you back and watching
from the cul de sac. Ash coated the windshield.
Power lines came down and mounds of asphalt
shingles melted to bare slabs. Our driveway's
caked with black glop only real tools will budge.
It looks like war. You said we'd never see
bad trouble here. But you swear e-mail is safe too.
Guess what? They called choppers to bombard
our house with red water and stood there ticking
boxes on clipboards when it burned out anyway.
Anyway, don't call my cell. I'll call you.

Horizon

after W. H. Auden

Men lieutenant
their sons, skins

signed for shields. Grief
loiters in another's boots.

Million-dollar machinery
flickers in desert fatigues.

Electronica, sweat,
and sweet shoulder meat.

First-class ships glide past
olive girls. The thin lipped

local help can't stomach air power.

Dream of Flight

Hook your toes in the aileron's groove.
Spill with the rivets down the runway.
It's a Monday, like every last Monday
on Earth. Time to check the satellite view.
Broad plains of depot roofs sprout metal cubes
between logos sketched with colored gravel.
Dusty circles of fallow orange soil
nestle in the cadastral grid of roads.
Where the scabrous crust of commerce quits,
asphalt ganglia splay out crisscrosswise
to the next irruption. No big surprise:
a flash flood of flesh syrups down the Strip.
On the mesa, a squad of trucks prattles,
blithe as tadpoles in a slickrock puddle.

Facing West

From Ponto Jetty north, high bluffs obscure
the lights of town and low surf sloshes piles
of kelp into mounds as lumpy as corpses.
It's dark enough at last to see tour boats
blinking on swells stacked up by offshore wind.
High tide will erase the ranger's tire tracks.
Curlews backlit by a yellow moon drill
for crabs burrowed into wave-rippled sand.
Rusty expansion bolts hold the seawalls down.
Rancid squid foul the beach. They must have flocked
to the highway's glow since bait fish never
balled up in the surf like normal this year.
The power station blinks at a line of jets:
tin cans hauling suits to runways downtown.

MEL>LAX
after Robert Creeley

This 747 is half empty.
Cranky execs and mums
gathered out of the bush fires
of Victoria are bound
for the bush fires of SoCal
where we build our kids
the same balloon-frame boxes
in the same eucalypt stands
that six months from now will offgas
the same aromatic oils
then explode when Santa Anas
drive crown fires to the Pacific.
A laid-off firie lit up
the Victoria bush
just like that broke hotshot
in Apache Junction.
Here we go back
bearing fur boots
and koala board books
so our kids won't clam up
at the baggage carousel.
A failed L.A. loan broker
drives the beverage cart
and scoffs at Australia's
single-payer plan. Here we go
back to the land of principled
cruelty and bleached teeth
always willing and able
to operate the emergency door.

Baghdad Swing
after Lorenzo Thomas

They scowled backpacking into Fallujah
and tuned out the babble of kids and clerks,
musing along the cemetery fence
before the pace of shelling picked up.
A battered Abrams clunked onto the field.
Baghdad was nowhere and nobody
was quiet anymore. Someday
the crowd will stop waiting.
Maybe grave hucksters selling
ancient wisdom will gossip
on the doorstep in back in Houston.
Maybe the Sunday papers
will deliver ten fat sections
orthodox as Deuteronomy.

Dream of Fog

She counts swells and paints the anchor blue.
I hoist mackerel into the bait well
and she coils eons of rope by the moon.
My notebook's clasped shut in the engine room.
We're bored as janitors bleaching old grout.
The yowling engine is still pissing steam
and even squinting we can't see the rimed
pilings in a slick of ions and meat.
A hank of old hose hangs on the deck rail
by a pail of trimmings and tentacles.
Sea oats root in the spall below the bluffs.
Scales glint like hoar on rigging and gunnels
and waste fish bob against the chine. Waves purl
where we bail, sick but primping for landfall.

Corrales Rancho Homes

After rain the clay hills smell like dishes
left for days. Cowboy engineers plugged
drainages and tractored terraced pads.
They felled oaks and left a fetch for sour wind.
Now puddles grow algae dumplings. Some days
the creeks run black with lumpy gravy.
For Sale signs mushroom and business
casual reps fleece the elders clean.
They rewrite the history of limestone.
Some leggy singer with a microphone
scatters dollar bills by the brick gate:
There's extra closets, girls, and lots of shelves!
No wind, no drought, no blight can hurt people
stacked in houses rooted deep as these.

Another Albuquerque Job

I'm back on the sun-stunned
cement at Lomas and Central
but not so young as once.
The old university
is flush with new money
and football banners.
This was our home ground:
the hokum of Old Town's
zocalo, the stuccoed
apartment complexes
between Lead and Coal.
Now the zoo's a biopark
and the Lobo theatre
sells micro-brews.
Sometimes it takes
more imagination
to come back than to leave.
From here to Amistad
on the Texas border
the Rio Grande dwindles
like a forgotten treaty.
Out past the country club,
footpaths thread through head-high
willows in the floodplain.
The finer the mesh
the quicker you disappear.
The West Mesa still sells old
tales of sprinklers and shade.
It's all uphill to Paradise
and all the talk is dark.
Who persecuted who.
What we did or didn't do.

Anza Borrego

I can't find my balance in the talus.

Playa.
>   Bajada.
>>   Decomposed granite.

The new pack bites my hips and shoulders.

Fishhook.
>   Teddy-bear cholla.
>>   Mojave claret cup.

A scouting raven spots me and croaks once.

Half-dead chamisa
>   drills into weathered schist
>>   and staghorns rot upright
>>>   leaving bundles of hollow stems.

A lone phainopepla sings in the allthorn.

My boots crunch
>   across caliche
>>   one and two
>>>   and one and two.

A fly lights in the sweat on my forehead.

Chert flakes and fire-cracked
>   rocks mark a Cahuilla site.
>>   A spring must be close by.

Five black-throated sparrows whistle in the smoke trees.

Beavertail cactus
>   glow purple with glochids
>>   in a low stone circle.

The creosote here wears spiky round galls
      and wind makes the lower branches sweep
            curved scars in the arroyo's white sand.

The sun falls behind the granite peaks of Buck Ridge.

Next to a salt-and-pepper boulder,
      there's an old ocotillo--its base at least a foot through--
            that divides all at once into fifty spiked branches.

I drop the pack and cook the soup and roll out my bed.

A half-moon backlights
      whorls of dime-sized leaves.
            Green pith glints through the bark
                like proud flesh through a scab.

At dawn, a house sparrow
      calls from the topmost raceme
            and ice crystals rattle in my jug.

Two potsherds rest
      in the white sand by my bed--
            domestic gray ware
                with thumb-nail ridges.

A luna moth drinks water from my cup.

Dream of Daughters

Judith is a creature of dusk who wakes
on an adolescent animal's clock.
She's famous for asking if food explains
how we die or hospitals how we live.
Miranda channels water on a screen
and delays the attack of sleep with games.
She plunges into her body at dawn,
just awake enough to swim to class.
Ariel loves the blast of hours but wakes
sullen in the dark. She's a sorceress
searching for a mammal's natural power
to spiral into the deeps, to weather
the deluge. She's a siphon, a grapple,
a tempest searching for a vacant shore.

Cerro de las Posas

A mob of graders scraped a pad on Double Peak.
They had to double up to get their blades to bite.
Now a spry guard in a prefab shed checks lumber
trucks and subcontractors through a chain link gate.
A beat-down Peterbilt hauling a flatbed
waits to drop four sections of concrete culvert.
The boss, in loafers and a hard hat, checks off
generators, concrete pumps, and backhoes.
A forklift unloads a dozen palms and rights
them between pallets of red roof tiles and studs.
Rigging cranes and cherry pickers bob and weave
through blade scars and clumps of eucalyptus slash.
Behind the hurricane fence, wild mustard,
mullein, and fennel sprout through hydroseed slop.

Convenience

Los indocumentados lock their bikes
to chain link behind the touchless carwash.
They line up in the lot like strikers
to flag down contractors for day work.
The mayor sends his driver through the line
for tortilla chips. His plump hand rolls
the window down and waves them over
with a pink *Financial Times*.
His fat head, topped with a wedge
of lacquered black hair,
lolls in a broadcloth collar.
He grunts and snuffles
in the big back seat, his face
as blank as a steak on a plate.

Commencement

He scraped his entry-level jowls
until they beamed like newborn ice

and zipped his naphtha-reeking robe
and donned his tam and stupid cowl.

Now he sits as stiff as glass, bored
as milk. He rules out more coffee.

He luffs in an ocean of gowns,
smiles at shoals of pie-eyed scholars.

Squirmy as frog eggs, the next crop
of elders sulk in gluey clumps.

In mortarboards, they look alike
as nails in noon's orderly light.

Dream of Frost in Boston

He arranges the andirons, sweeps the slate
hearth, reclines, and crosses his heavy boots,
then he plucks a chocolate from the brass plate
and finds, once more, the candy covers fruit.
He drums against his thigh, flushes, goes dumb,
lurches for words to speak his latest thought,
and reckons his routine helps him keep from
needing to recall the names that he's forgot.
Sodden with slurs and halts, his heavy voice
drifts as he dredges for words. Why the weird
tic: hedging when our talk turns to his faults?
It must remain from when he was revered.
An old hunger for rhyme, once honed on slang,
has dwindled to a dull, but constant, pang.

After the Fires
after Robert Lowell

Our North County streets clog
with drifts of ash. Sound walls
and Saltillo pots shine with dust.

Outside our little shops, computerized
sprinklers whisper as we edge
ice plant and behead pagan weeds.

We amble down the rain-smooth stairs
at D Street. Our pride cools in wet sand
and we grunt at the democracy of kelp.

Fall Canyon

Sink your feet
      into the black sand
            of a tragedy or two.

The idea of a desert spills
      from mesquite blossoms on the wind.

Under a new moon
      a coyote steers
            by wellhead gas flares

bearing a road-killed
      woodrat to pups denned
            between tanks of crude.

The sweep of dry air in creosote.
      It can help to lie.

The best guide to time is a mesa
      high above a silky dune
            where I keep the gift of my death.

Variations on My Life
after Lyn Hejinian

1

A bit of flesh, enamel, and cloth,
    a child,
        looked at me like history.
Papa seated at the wheel,
    book worn,
        polished bald.
A tired landscape
    beckoning to a little thing
        who sings a laugh.

I link to a picture after every war.
    Always a beach
        with chirping and trills
where birds won't harm my marigolds.
    Trees smile and look there,
        it's 1969!
How could I ever have wondered
    that such and such
        is art?

And who needs aging?
    Time was
        anyone might have been magic
since airport time is normative,
    more a freedom
        than a shore.
When your flight approaches
    and you are done to order
        you can arrange it all from there.

How can anyone find astrology interesting
    when the apple
        is in the pie?

We work for love,
      for those who people
            the silence when the radio breaks.
There is no solitude
      with carrots, radishes, and beans.
            Little silences hum between the big ones.

2

His daughter wanted a grammar
where you can still speak when it's gone.

He insisted she learn history
and reason out lines of verse.

He notified the agent of their plans
though vacations troubled his German side.

Her ice cubes melted in order and she took
to tapping, as restless as a bottle of pop.

She lacked the patience for landscapes
but her window gave her views of little airplanes.

She was dreaming of an alternative
to the triumphant bourgeoisie's artful disarray.

Her song was too sweet in the original
but little sirens went off in translation.

She waited for the future perfect then spilled
the sugar: Goodbye will have been enough.

He knew a man would know something
on the dot if he saw her there at the sill.

At daylight threadbare sparrows kept telling her
of dusty grass and the lilac smell of rust.

She followed the notes to a tenor
practicing in the next street over.

They proceeded to the hidden monument
and drove through a well-lit tunnel.

She sang out the window that nature is garbage.
She couldn't see a collision at their speed.

    3

From chard and tomatoes
        by a judicious tree,
from peas and garlic
        by the abundant sea,
she chalks down order
        and determines the nature of progress.

She is quite the child of immovable fact.
        Elephants at the circus are solid.
The rings are clotted with their knees.
        Despite the familiarity of roses
and the certainty of matter,
        she lingers on the birds.

In her search for a hidden city
        on a coast that never goes dark
she circles back and loops wide
        where the headland turns the river,
where everything is boardwalk
        and the dark is flowering shrubs.

Her sleepy father stands at the rail
        and dreams of a worn-out suit

and the larger cars we drove at the time.
>Only now of course comes
the comic satisfaction of knowing
>there was nothing he could have done.

On her more faithless days she says
>There are some sights still surprising:
robins worming in the goldenrod,
>a lull in the activity of clouds,
the old apothecary filling a jar
>in a fit of comprehension.

She juggles sheep for sleep
>and apples for good luck.
She does have a compulsion.
>For eight years or so
the distance was birds
>and every bird was really a word.

NOTES

"Horizon" remixes W. H. Auden's "The Shield of Achilles."

"Facing West" alludes to Walt Whitman's "Facing West from California's Shores."

"MEL > LAX" responds to Robert Creeley's "The Dogs of Auckland."

"Baghdad Swing" responds to Lorenzo Thomas's "Morning Raga."

"Dream of Daughters" alludes to William Shakespeare's *The Tempest.*

"After the Fires" is a negative image of Robert Lowell's "For the Union Dead."

"Variations on My Life" remixes sections of Lyn Hejinian's *My Life.*

Lance Newman is the author of *Proverbs of Earth* (Spuyten Duyvil Press, 2025), as well as two chapbooks: *3by3by3* (Beard of Bees, 2010) and *Come Kanab* (Dusie, 2007). His poems have appeared in magazines in the US, the UK, and Australia. Newman teaches literature, media, and writing at Westminster University in Salt Lake City, Utah. For more information, see http://www.lancenewman.org

www.ingramcontent.com/pod-product-compliance
Lightning Source LLC
Chambersburg PA
CBHW022053080426
42734CB00009B/1327